Encounters with Jesus

seven gospel stories imagined

by Anna Rapa

da[w]bar house

ISBN-13: 978-0-9887573-0-1
ISBN-10: 0988757303

Cover design by Dave Malec © 2013

Table of Contents

What is Encounters with Jesus?

Through these seven stories, you will be invited to imagine what it was like to encounter Jesus while he was here on earth. Each story is told from the perspective of someone who met Jesus. These people will tell you, in their own words, what their lives were like before Jesus, how they encountered Jesus, and how Jesus changed their lives.

Encounter Jesus with Friends

The stories can be used by individuals who follow Jesus to start discussions with other people who are spiritually interested. They give a great jumping off point for spiritual discussions, and most importantly, they allow Jesus to introduce himself in his own words and actions as they appear in Scripture.

Encounter Jesus with Small Groups

These stories are designed to be read aloud to a group and then discussed in the oral storying tradition. Storying is a return to the stories of Scripture as narratives. The goal is for people to imaginatively listen and experience the stories like they were there. In this way, the process is similar to Lectio Divina.

Appendix 2 contains a leader's guide with lesson planning information and some teaching notes.

Nicodemus

I can't say I was surprised when they kicked me off the Ruling Council. I really can't. I hoped it wouldn't come to that, but I sort of expected that it might. It's a long story though. Are you sure you want to hear it?

Alright, well, here's how it went down. It was basically like any other year, right? Day after day, it was the same kind of thing. A man would come to us about how his neighbor had planted something in his field. A husband would come to us wanting permission to divorce his wife. You know, normal stuff. And then there were the more interesting cases–boy, could it get intense when all 70 of us were gathered together to argue about one point of law or another. Our main goal was to keep the peace among the people, to make sure that we were still walking according to the laws that our fathers laid down, and to keep people prepared for and awaiting the Messiah.

3

Oh, you probably don't know about the Messiah . . . . Well, there are old prophecies, you see, in the old books, that talk about the rescue of Israel from its oppressors. We had been waiting for more than 400 years for this Messiah to come. We were expecting that he would come any day to free us from the Romans and give us back our own land. We were always on the lookout for who it would be. But many days it seemed like the Messiah would never come–would never hear the cries of his people and come to rescue us.

Anyway, we started hearing these rumblings about a man named Jesus. He was stirring up a lot of conversation. Even when we were just hanging out, not holding council meetings, Jesus's name came up. We heard claims that he had turned water into wine at a wedding feast. Crazy, right? I mean, why would anyone even do that? Then there was this guy, a prophet named John, and he actually claimed that this Jesus was the Son of God! Can you believe it? Others said that he healed the sick. They also claimed that he could cast out demons.

4

But what really got people upset was when Jesus came to the temple during Passover. Instead of celebrating with the rest of the community, something happened to make him angry. Someone told me his face turned beet red, and he actually shouted. He knocked over tables in the temple marketplace, and he made a whip and drove all the merchants from the temple courts. Can you believe that? I mean, who did he think he was? We'd been selling things that way for hundreds of years. Why should we change it now? At least that's what my colleagues thought.

We talked about that little incident for days. Even then, some were arguing that Jesus should be held back and prevented from speaking. But others stood up for him and said that he couldn't be performing these kinds of miraculous signs unless he was sent from God.

So anyway, all this talk made me kind of intrigued. I'm not one to rock the boat normally, but in this case, I thought I should at least investigate. Why not just go to Jesus and have a conversation with him? Just see what he was saying? People had told me that he said such strange things that I guess I just wanted to see for myself.

I have to admit, though, I was a little bit nervous. The Council is powerful, and I really didn't want to cross anyone. But I just had to go and see him. So one night when Jesus was nearby, I went and found him after dark. Our conversation went like this:

"Rabbi, we know you are a teacher who has come from God. For no one could perform the miraculous signs you are doing if God were not with him."✝

Jesus replied, "Very truly I tell you, no one can see the kingdom of God unless they are born again."✝

"How can someone be born when they are old?" I asked. "Surely they cannot return a second time to their mother's womb to be born!"✝

"Very truly I tell you, no one can enter the kingdom of God unless they are born of water and

6

the Spirit. Flesh gives birth to flesh, but the Spirit gives birth to spirit. You should not be surprised by my saying, 'You must be born again.' The wind blows wherever it pleases. You hear its sound, but you cannot tell where it came from or where it is going. So it is with everyone born of the Spirit."†

At this point, I was really confused. "How can this be?"† I asked.

Jesus seemed shocked. He said, "You are Israel's teacher, and do you not understand these things? Very truly I tell you, we speak of what we know, and we testify to what we have seen, but still you people do not accept our testimony. I have told you of earthly things and you do not believe; how then will you believe if I speak of heavenly things? No one has ever gone into heaven except the one who came from heaven–the Son of Man. Just as Moses lifted up the snake in the wilderness, so the Son of Man must be lifted up, [so that everyone who believes in him may have life with the Eternal One through him.]"†

And then he turned and walked away. And

I just sat down, on a tree stump, and thought for a long time. Those people must have been right when they said that John the Baptizer called him the Son of God. Now Jesus had called himself the Son of Man–to me . . . to my face. Did he know what he was doing? Claiming to be the Messiah, the one who would rescue Israel? The one that we had been waiting for for hundreds of years? And he made that claim in front me–one of the members of the Ruling Council!

If it wasn't true, if it couldn't be verified, then he could be put to death under our laws for blasphemy. And yet he seemed unconcerned about that; he was only shocked that I didn't already know who he was.

I shook my head, and I thought some more. I thought again about all the stories of him healing people and rescuing them from demons. It wouldn't really have been possible to do that without God being with him. So I went back to the Council the next day, and I went to our records of the old writings. I spent days poring over them.

And I began to think that we might have been wrong about what we expected the Messiah to be.

We'd expected that he would come in military strength and power. We'd expected that he would lead a military campaign and crush the Roman oppressors. We'd even celebrated him as the Messiah when he rode into the city on a donkey shortly before the Passover that year. We thought that deliverance was near.

Later, when he died, we were heartbroken. I got close enough to the disciples during that time to know that they were feeling just as disappointed and lost as I was. They didn't always understand what Jesus was talking about, but they had placed their faith in him. They trusted that he was going to rescue us. None of us expected him to die.

But I think that Jesus knew that he was going to die and tried to prepare us. He even tried to prepare me, when he compared himself to the snake in the wilderness. See, my people were stuck in the desert, wandering around, and complaining against God, claiming that he was not taking care of them.

So then snakes came and were biting and poisoning people, and the people repented. God told Moses to make a bronze snake and lift it up. And he told Moses that anyone who looked at the snake would live. I think Jesus was trying to prepare us for the fact that he really was different than we expected, that he would die in the way that he did, and that his death would be the remedy to the brokenness we experience.

Because ultimately, he didn't just die–he also rose from the grave! Before that, I really did believe that he came from God. But it was only after he arose and appeared to his disciples that I believed that he was the Messiah. And I finally understood that he expected to free us–not from the bonds of Roman oppression, but from the bonds of our own brokenness and our inability to walk with God.

I saw it time and time again, as one of the rulers of the Council. Every day, people were breaking the law and fighting and bickering and hurting one another. We were not able to live up to the ideal–to the perfection that was laid out for us in the Torah, our holy writings.

But when I put my faith in Jesus, something changed. It's not that I was perfect. But I was able to walk with God in a different way. I was able to trust him to make me clean, and I could walk with him, the Eternal One. I didn't have to worry about keeping the law anymore–I didn't have to work to make myself perfect to approach God. All I had to do was think about walking according to the principles Jesus taught and living within the abundant life that Jesus talked about.

And that's when I got kicked out of the Council. Because most of the Jews didn't believe that Jesus is the Messiah. They're still waiting for someone to rescue us politically. And I just couldn't keep my mouth shut. What Jesus said about the spirit and being born again was right! I am a whole new man. And I wanted to tell other people about the change in my life. So that's what I'm doing now. I'm just a poor man, with no status and no power. But I am a happy man. I am content with my life. And in my old age, I have found what it means to walk with the Eternal One.

_____

✝ Quotations taken from John 3.
You can read Nicodemus's story in John 3.

Discussion Questions

- What did you notice about this story?
- What did you wonder about?

- What have you heard about Jesus?
- What expectations do you have about who he is or what he does in a person's life?
- Where did these expectations come from?
- Do you think that they are right or wrong?

- What has the church told you about Jesus?
- What do you think the church is getting wrong about Jesus?

- Do you think the Bible is trustworthy?
- If not, where else can you look for information about Jesus?
- Do you know anyone who knows Jesus?
- What questions do you have for them?

- What do you think life with the Eternal One looks like?
- How would you find that life? How would you start it?
- Jesus referred to being born of the Spirit. What do you think that means?
- How do you think that a life lived with the Eternal One would be similar to the life you're living right now?
- How might it be different?

What questions do you have for Jesus? Write or
draw them below.

The Woman at the Well

Today I'll have been married
for ten years. *Ten* years. It's an
eternity compared to . . . well . . .
compared to my life before. But a lot
has changed, and ten years doesn't seem so
impossible now.

Jeremiah is actually my sixth husband. Does
that shock you? I know it's an awful lot. But there
were always reasons to divorce that seemed so good
at the time. You know that I couldn't actually
divorce them, of course. The law didn't allow it.
But there are ways; there are ways. And I just
couldn't help but be drawn away when a new man
showed interest in me.

The first time, I don't know what it was
about me that drew him in. I was minding my own
business with all the other women in town. But
somehow, he must have known the attention my
heart hungered for, and I couldn't resist. Once it
happened once, and I was divorced from the first

husband and on to the second, my reputation was settled. From there on out, I got lots of attention from all the seedy men in town. So one after the other, I was seduced, divorced, and moved on.

I can't deny my own responsibility though–not now. I know that I had choices to make, even then, about faithfulness to my vows. I can't explain it to you except to say that I was hungering for something that I couldn't find. I always hoped that the next man would be the answer.

In a way, a man did provide me with the answer. But it wasn't any answer I'd ever thought to look for. And I'm not talking about Jeremiah now.

It was a really hot day. By this time, I was avoiding meeting with other women in town. I used to spend all my time with them–gathering water, washing clothes, preparing food. You know . . . the things women do. But by the time I made it to husband number three, I wasn't really welcome. It's not like they were overtly cruel to me. I would just catch someone staring, or conversation would stop the moment I walked up. And they certainly kept the younger girls away from me. They didn't want whatever it was that I had to rub off on their precious children. So it became easier to just make my own way. I began to avoid gathering with anyone in town. I became really lonely. And cynical. I doubted that anyone could actually truly care about me at all.

So anyway, it was a hot day. I usually tried to gather water early in the morning, just after the women left. But for some reason, that day I had other things going on. So I didn't get to the well until about noon. And there was this guy just sitting there. He looked exhausted, and he was sitting there, in the sun. As I approached, he was leaning back against a stone, his arm flung over his forehead, sort of shading his eyes. I thought his eyes were closed, so I went around to the other side of the well. I was trying to avoid all manner of questionable situations. By this time, I'd met Jeremiah. Though we weren't married, he treated me differently than all the men before. I knew that he loved me, and I didn't want to jeopardize it.

So I was attaching my rope to the skin I'd brought to draw water when I heard the man's voice.

"Will you give me a drink?"†

I looked over at him, and he was staring straight at me. His eyes were kind. He didn't look at me the way the men in town did, like I was an object for his own pleasure. His eyes didn't waver from my face as he waited for the answer. I was accustomed to being treated poorly by men, and I noticed he was a Jew from the way that he dressed, so I didn't immediately offer him the hospitality I should have.

"You are a Jew and I am a Samaritan woman. How can *you* ask *me* for a drink?"†

It was odd that he did, actually. Most Jews that I had encountered would never drink from the same skin as a Samaritan. They were so angry that we didn't accept all of their holy books and that we disagreed with them about how to properly worship God. So anyway, it seemed like a reasonable objection. But he responded very strangely.

"If you knew the gift of God and who it is that asks you for a drink, you would have asked him and he would have given you living water."†

"Sir," I said, "you have nothing to draw with and the well is deep. Where can you get this living water? Are you greater than our father Jacob, who gave us the well and drank from it himself, as did also his sons and his livestock?"†

The man answered, "Everyone who drinks this water will be thirsty again, but whoever drinks the water I give them will never thirst. Indeed, the water I give them will become in them a spring of water welling up to [life with the Eternal One.]"†

I hesitated for just a second, and then I said, "Sir, give me this water so that I won't get thirsty and have to keep coming here to draw water."† You see, it would've solved a lot of problems for me if I didn't have to keep coming back to the well in the middle of the day like that. But then it got even weirder.

"Go, call your husband and come back," he said.†

"I have no husband," I replied.†

"You are right when you say you have no husband. The fact is, you have had five husbands, and the man you now have is not your husband. What you have just said is quite true."†

I was shocked. And horrified. How did this man know all about me? He hadn't even set foot in our town. Although I might have looked tired, disheveled, even coarse, he could not have known the actual number of my former husbands without special knowledge from God. But I didn't wish to talk about my sordid history. So I tried a diversion. I recognized that he must be a prophet, so I asked him about where we should be worshiping–on the mountain in Samaria, like my people believed, or in Jerusalem, like the Jews believed.

He replied, "Woman, believe me, a time is coming when you will worship the Father neither on this mountain nor in Jerusalem. You Samaritans worship what you do not know; we worship what

20

we do know, for salvation is from the Jews. Yet a time is coming and has now come when the true worshipers will worship the Father in the Spirit and in truth, for they are the kind of worshipers the Father seeks. God is spirit, and his worshipers must worship in the Spirit and in truth."†

It was then that I began to suspect that he was the one who was prophesied about–the one who would teach and explain everything to us Samaritans. So I said, "I know that Messiah is coming. When he comes, he will explain everything to us."†

And he said, "I, the one speaking to you—I am he."†

Just then, a group of men approached us. They seemed to know the man. So I left abruptly, leaving my water skin behind. I started out walking back toward town, thinking about all that the man had said. It was then that I realized that the water he was offering wasn't real water at all–it was something else. Could it be that which I had been seeking all this time? He had mentioned life with the Eternal One . . . could that be what I was missing? As I thought about it, I started walking faster and faster. By the time I reached the town, I was running and calling out to the townspeople– "Come, you have to meet this man . . . he told me everything I ever did. Could he be the Messiah?" I didn't even hesitate. I ran right to the gates of the city where the important men sat. And then I went to the river where the women were gathered and told them too. I must have made quite a spectacle, because many followed me back to the well.

When we arrived, the townspeople invited Jesus to stay in town for a couple of days. He did, and he taught us many things about becoming his followers. If you can believe it, he actually invited us, Samaritans, to become his disciples. Many in town decided to follow him. They even began to call him the Savior of the world.

So that was the day that my life changed. I couldn't get enough of Jesus's words. I spent every moment of those two days with Jesus, listening to him explain things. I dragged Jeremiah along, and we both were transformed.

When Jesus used the picture of living water, I think he did that on purpose. As we talked more during his stay, I saw that the life he was inviting us to was one of celebration, abundance, joy, unpredictability, fruitfulness. I think of lush green plants and rich and diverse animal life, and I think that we are invited into life the way it was meant to be. Jesus explained that we could have this life through him. It was the life I'd always wanted. What was even more amazing is that he offered this life now. Unlike the teachings I'd grown up hearing, which promised a wonderful life after the final resurrection, Jesus was offering this life in the here and now.

Shortly after that, Jeremiah and I were married, and we've been together ever since. When we learned of Jesus's death, we were heartbroken. But we heard the news that he had risen from the dead, and we traveled to meet with his disciples. We have been living among them ever since.

† Quotations taken from John 4.

The woman's story about meeting Jesus is found in John 4. Her story of what happened to her after Jesus stayed in her town is pure conjecture. There is no biblical evidence that the woman ever got married to the man she was living with or that she joined Jesus's disciples after he died and was raised again.

Discussion Questions

- What did you notice about this story?
- What did you wonder about?

- What do you think the woman was looking for?
- Why do you think she was looking for it in men?
- Why do you think she didn't find it there?

- What was the life that Jesus was offering? How was it different from the life offered by the other men in the woman's life?
- How do you think that the woman was to take hold of the life Jesus was offering?
- How do you think she was supposed to learn about that life?

- Jesus said, "True worshipers will worship me in spirit and in truth." What does it mean to worship someone?
- What did it mean that Jesus said that people would worship him? According to Jewish culture, who deserved worship?
- What does it mean that God is seeking out worshipers?
- What does a life of worship look like? Do you think it's similar to or different from life with the Eternal One?

What are you looking for that you haven't been able to find? Do you think Jesus is able to provide those things for you?

The Blind Man

At first, all I heard was a crowd. It was big, from the sounds of it. Babies crying, people yelling at one another through the marketplace, and the constant dull thumping of feet against the dirt. As they approached, I couldn't quite make out their conversation. There was a group of them that seemed to be arguing about something. Finally they came right up to me, and I heard someone ask, "Rabbi, who sinned, this man or his parents, that he was born blind?"†

Oh, I definitely wanted to hear the answer to this one! So I raised my eyebrow and turned my face toward them.

"Neither this man nor his parents sinned," said the rabbi, "but this happened so that the works of God might be displayed in him. As long as it is day, we must do the works of him who sent me. Night is coming, when no one can work. While I am in the world, I am the light of the world."†

I nodded my head. That's right. It wasn't my fault I was born blind. How could I have sinned before I was even born? I suppose it could've been my parents' fault, but the rabbi didn't seem to think so.

And then I heard someone spit. The person leaned down to the ground and started moving the dirt around. All of a sudden, I felt one of the man's hands on my shoulders. And then I felt him pressing a plaster of dirt and spit onto one eye. He bent again to the ground and then did the other eye.

And then I heard, "Go, wash in the pool of Siloam."†

I turned my face toward him for a second, wondering. And then I heard someone shout "Jesus!" and the group began to walk away. Hmm, even more interesting. I'd heard about this guy before. He was getting a reputation for stirring up trouble. And . . . for healing people.

Healing people? Did he heal me?

I jumped to my feet and left my cup on the side of the road. With my hands extended, I went as fast as I could to the pool of Siloam. As I raced there, I called out for directions, "Which way to the pool of Siloam? Which way?"

Finally, I made it through the crowds and found the pool. But instead of running and splashing headlong into the pool, I paused. This was the moment of truth. Had he really healed me? What if I washed off the mud and was just as blind as before? But what if I could see? In the end, I decided I had nothing to lose. So I washed the mud off and opened my eyes. And I could see! I could see!

I ran home and began telling everyone around me that I could see. My neighbors didn't all believe me. Some agreed that I was the man who was born blind. But others doubted it. I just kept saying, "It is me. I am the blind man, but now I can see." They asked me how it happened, and I told them that the man called Jesus had spit on some mud, rubbed it on my eyes, and that was that.

So my neighbors brought me to the Pharisees. The Pharisees were concerned that this happened on a Sabbath day, so they repeated the question, "How did you receive your sight?"

"He put mud on my eyes," I replied, "and I washed, and now I see."†

This spurred a huge argument. Some of them claimed that he could not have been from God because he did this on the Sabbath and it is against God's law to heal anyone on the Sabbath unless they are in mortal danger. But others wondered how a man could heal someone born blind unless the man was from God.

So they turned again and asked me, "What have you to say about him? It was your eyes he opened."†

I said, "He is a prophet."†

So then they sent for my parents. They still weren't sure that I was really born blind and had really been healed. My parents must have realized what all the controversy was about and were afraid of being kicked out of the synagogue. So when the Pharisees asked them about how I was healed, they said, "We know he is our son, and we know he was born blind. But how he can see now, or who opened his eyes, we don't know. Ask him. He is of age; he will speak for himself."✝

So again, they asked me, "Give glory to God by telling the truth. We know this man is a sinner."✝

By now I was getting aggravated. They simply didn't want to believe what had happened to me. So, with my new sight, I looked them straight in the eyes, one by one, and said, "Whether he is a sinner or not, I don't know. One thing I do know. I was blind but now I see!"✝

Then they asked, "What did he do to you? How did he open your eyes?"✝

"I have told you already and you did not listen. Why do you want to hear it again? Do you want to become his disciples too?"✝

I might have gone too far there, making fun of them, but after what happened next, I wasn't sorry. They turned on me and said, "You are this fellow's disciple! We are disciples of Moses! We know that God spoke to Moses, but as for this fellow, we don't even know where he comes from."†

I said, "Now that is remarkable! You don't know where he comes from, yet he opened my eyes. We know that God does not listen to sinners. He listens to the godly person who does his will. Nobody has ever heard of opening the eyes of a man born blind. If this man were not from God, he could do nothing."†

And then they said that I was steeped in sin at birth, and they threw me out.

Well, now I was angry. Jesus had already said that it wasn't because of my sin that I was born blind. And I think he was right. Those Pharisees were just worried that Jesus was going to take all their religious power away from them. It wasn't really fair, them kicking me out like that, just because I was defending Jesus.

So I decided I would walk around town and see all the things I had never seen before. It was amazing to put the awesome colors and other sights together with the sounds and feelings that I had experienced my whole life. Then I walked over to my old corner to see the place where I had sat to beg for all those years. It was there Jesus found me again.

He asked me, "Do you believe in the Son of Man?"†

The Son of Man? He was talking about the Messiah? The one we had been waiting for all these years? So I asked, "Who is he, sir? Tell me so that I may believe in him."†

He said, "You have now seen him; in fact, he is the one speaking with you."†

I said, "Lord, I believe."† And then I bowed down and worshiped him.

Jesus turned to his followers and said, "For judgment I have come into this world, so that the blind will see and those who see will become blind."†

Some Pharisees were standing there and asked him, "What? Are we blind too?"†

Jesus looked at them and said, "If you were blind, you would not be guilty of sin; but now that you claim you can see, your guilt remains."†

So the day I got my sight, I found more than the world around me. I found the Messiah. From that day on, I never stopped telling my story to anyone who would listen.

_____

† Quotations taken from John 9.

This story is found in John 9.

Discussion Questions

- What did you notice about this story?
- What did you wonder about?

- What do you think the blind man felt like when Jesus put mud on his face?
- What do you think it was like to run through town looking for the pool, wondering if he was healed?
- What do you think that moment of truth was like, when he opened his eyes for the first time?
- Why do you think Jesus asked him to go and wash instead of just healing him outright?
- What do you think would have happened if the man had not gone to the pool to wash?

- What do you think of the community's response to the man?
- What did the controversy seem to be about?
- What was the significance of healing on the Sabbath?
- Why do you think the man's parents wouldn't commit to saying anything about Jesus?

- What did the man say about Jesus? How did that change over time?
- Why do you think the man bowed down and worshiped Jesus when Jesus said he was the

Son of Man?
- Why didn't Jesus stop him from worshiping?
- How did that compare or contrast to the religion of the Jews?

- Why do you think that Jesus came back to find the man that was blind? What does that tell us about Jesus?

- What do you think about what Jesus said about blindness to the Pharisees? What kind of blindness do you think he was talking about?

What do Jesus's claims about being the Messiah mean to you? If you believed he was the Messiah, how would that change your life?

The Rich Young Ruler

It's too much. It's just too much. I want to do what he asked me, I really do. But he asked me for the one thing I can't give.

I've been a good man all my life. I was successful enough in my studies and in my business that they made me a member of the Ruling Council, even though I was young. I guess they could see that I followed the law and did all the right things.

But I often wondered–was that enough? I mean–was it really enough? I got really concerned about it. What if there was something more I should be doing? It seemed like there should be more. I mean, I keep the Ten Commandments–I don't worship other gods or make images of them; I don't take God's name in vain, don't lie, don't steal, and don't commit adultery.   I don't give false testimony, and I don't covet. I honor my father and mother and keep the Sabbath day. Every single one of these commands I've kept since I was young. Not many people can do that. Even so, I wanted to be sure of my place in the faith, and I wanted to be sure of what would happen to me after death.

So Jesus is in town. We've been talking about him quite a bit at the Council meetings. He's that rabbi, the son of Joseph that has quite a following. He's been making outlandish statements and stirring up trouble. But he also has a tendency to make a difference in people's lives. People claim that he's been healing the sick and making blind men see. And people are saying that he's been sent by God.

So I thought it might be a good idea to ask him about it. I didn't have anything to lose, and if he really is from God, then I thought I'd have a lot to gain.

So I heard he was in town and I spent today trying to find him. I looked for quite a while, and then I finally saw the crowd around him. I pushed my way through, and I threw myself at his feet.

"Good teacher, what must I do to inherit eternal life?"†

Jesus replied, "Why do you call me good? No one is good—except God alone."†

And then he started to answer my question. "You know the commandments: 'You shall not commit adultery, you shall not murder, you shall not steal, you shall not give false testimony, honor your father and mother.'"†

I replied, "All these I have kept since I was a boy."†

And then Jesus said, "You still lack one thing. Sell everything you have and give to the poor, and you will have treasure in heaven. Then come, follow me."†

Sell everything? Everything? I'm wealthy; I have so many things, and I live a comfortable life. Jesus roams from one city to another, imposing on the hospitality of others. I give hospitality to others. How can I give that up? Treasure in heaven sounds great, but how do I know that I'll really have it? And how does that help my life today? And just think about how many people I'm able to help and all the things that I can do for the poor. I can't give that up, can I?

Really, how can he ask so much of me? I've done everything that God has ever commanded. I am living a good life, according to the law. And what about Abraham? And Solomon? They had riches so far beyond mine, and God didn't ask them to give up their wealth. How can God possibly expect more of me?

No, I can't do it. I just can't do it. It's too much. And I refuse to believe that it's necessary for me to sell everything to follow God.

Jesus must have known what I was thinking, because he looked at me and said, "How hard it is for the rich to enter the kingdom of God! Indeed, it is easier for a camel to go through the eye of a needle than for someone who is rich to enter the kingdom of God."†

The people around him asked, "Who then can be saved?"†

Jesus answered, "What is impossible with man is possible with God."†

And that's when I left. I am heartbroken

41

about it, but there it is. I trust that God will reward me for my righteous living, even though I haven't sold everything I own.

---

† Quotations taken from Luke 18.

The full story can be found in Matthew 19, Mark 10, and Luke 18.

Discussion Questions

- What did you notice about this story?
- What did you wonder about?

- Why do you think Jesus reacted to the man's statement that he was good? What point do you think Jesus was trying to make?

- What did you notice about how the man defined his life of faith? Do you think he was right or wrong?
- How did Jesus challenge his perception?
- Why did Jesus ask him to sell all his possessions and give to the poor?
- Do you think that was a lot to ask?
- What do you think held the man back?
- What do you think he would have gained if he'd chosen to do what Jesus said?

- How does his story compare to the blind man's story? Do you think that what Jesus asked him to do was easier or harder than what he asked the blind man to do?

- What kind of life was Jesus inviting the man into? What do you think that life would have looked like for the man?
- What does it mean to "believe" in Jesus? Does it require more than thoughts? Does it require actions? What kind of actions?

What kind of life is Jesus inviting you into? What are you holding back from him?

Martha

My brother Lazarus died recently, for a second time.

The story's an interesting one–at least I think it's interesting. You see, Jesus was a close friend of mine. He was close to me, my sister Mary, and my brother Lazarus. And somehow we ended up near the center of the controversy that Jesus always seemed to stir up.

Maybe I should go back to the beginning though, shortly after we'd met him. He ended up coming over to my home, for a meal. It was an exciting time for us, but it was also really stressful. There are so many details that a woman has to worry about when she's hosting. And hosting Jesus! Well, that takes it to a whole other level. So anyway, I was racing around like a chicken with its head cut off, trying to get everything ready. Mary was very little help. She's prone to daydreaming anyway, but when she heard Jesus was coming, she was useless! She was supposed to be cleaning up the dining area, and I walked through five times while she was just standing in the same place, wiping down a table.

Anyway, I had just gotten the last item in place when Jesus and his followers knocked on the door. From then on, I was busy serving people food and drink and making sure everyone was taken care of. At one point, I got very upset. And this is embarrassing, but I think you should know the whole story. But I was upset because Mary wasn't helping me at all. And where do you think she was? Sitting at Jesus's feet, just listening to everything he had to say. Not only was it unusual for a woman to be in a dining room with men, it was unheard of for her to be seated at his feet, like a disciple. But this was one of the most amazing things. When I complained to Jesus that she wasn't helping me, this is what he said:

"Martha, Martha, you are worried and upset about many things, but few things are needed—or indeed only one. Mary has chosen what is better, and it will not be taken away from her."†

Just like that, he put me in my place. But Jesus didn't relegate me to the kitchen like other teachers would have. No, our place, mine and Mary's, was at his feet, as disciples. What an extraordinary thing!

Our relationship continued then. We learned many things from Jesus, and I believe we became special friends. And then our brother Lazarus died. We sent word to Jesus right away, but he didn't come until Lazarus had already been buried for four days. Four long days. We had the funeral, and we wrapped Lazarus's body, and we placed him in the tomb. We were in the middle of our week of mourning, and Mary was taking it very hard. She takes everything to heart.

So on the fourth day after Lazarus was buried, I heard that Jesus had returned to town. So I ran out to meet him. I marched right up to him and I said, "Lord, if you had been here, my brother would not have died. But I know that even now God will give you whatever you ask."††

Jesus replied, "Your brother will rise again."††

I said, "I know he will rise again in the resurrection at the last day."††

And then Jesus said, "I am the resurrection and the life. The one who believes in me will live, even though they die; and whoever lives by believing in me will never die. Do you believe this?"††

"Yes, Lord," I said, "I believe that you are the Messiah, the Son of God, who is to come into the world."††

After that, I ran to get my sister. I pulled her out of the house and told her that Jesus was there. When we left the house, all the people followed. When Mary got to the edge of the village, where Jesus was, she ran up to him and flung herself at his feet, weeping. "Lord," she sobbed, "if you had been here, my brother would not have died."††

Jesus asked to be shown where Lazarus was laid, and then he wept. People were amazed at how much he loved Lazarus, but some were saying that he should have kept Lazarus from dying.

Jesus ordered that the stone be rolled away from the tomb's opening. I objected, of course, "But, Lord, by this time there is a bad odor, for he has been there four days."††

And he said to me, "Did I not tell you that if you believe, you will see the glory of God?"††

So the people got the stone out of the way, and Jesus prayed, "Father, I thank you that you have heard me. I knew that you always hear me, but I said this for the benefit of the people standing here, that they may believe that you sent me."††

And then he looked at the tomb, and he said in the strongest voice I have ever heard, "Lazarus, come out!"††

And he did! My brother came out, wrapped in grave clothes. We couldn't even see his face. But he was there, and he was alive!

From that day on, people started talking about killing Lazarus. And they kept talking about killing Jesus too.

We had many more meals with Jesus. Instead of serving them, I, too, sat at Jesus's feet to listen. Shortly before Jesus was crucified, Mary poured out a whole year's worth of expensive oil on Jesus's feet. I think it was her way of showing how extravagantly she loved Jesus.

We were among those who mourned Jesus's death and who celebrated his resurrection from the dead. My sister and I love to tell the stories of those resurrections. Jesus's resurrection from the dead and his power over death is even sweeter to us now that Lazarus is dead again and we have to look forward to the final resurrection to be reunited with him and with Jesus.

----

† Quotations taken from Luke 10.

†† Quotations taken from John 11.

Martha's story can be found in Luke 10 and John 11.

Discussion Questions

- What did you notice about this story?
- What did you wonder about?

- What did you think about Mary's and Martha's different approaches to Jesus?
- Do you think that Martha was asking Jesus to heal her brother Lazarus?
- Do you think she believed that he would raise Lazarus from the dead?
- What about Mary? Why do you think she threw herself at Jesus's feet?
- Why do you think Jesus allowed women to be his disciples, even though that wasn't normal for the culture?

- Why do you think Jesus resurrected Lazarus?
- What do you think Lazarus's resurrected life was like?
- What do you think it means that Jesus had the power to do that?

- What do you think this adds to your understanding of life and death?
- What does it add to your understanding of spiritual life and death?
- How do you think Jesus knew that God would raise Lazarus from the dead when he prayed to God?

Describe or draw a picture of your spiritual existence. Is it alive or dead? Invite Jesus to bring abundant spiritual life to you.

Zacchaeus

Becoming a tax collector was not an easy decision. My people hated the Romans, and we rejected their right to rule over us. Our nation was just biding its time to rise up against our oppressors, to stand for the Holy One of Israel, the God of our Fathers. We were waiting for the Messiah to come.

But the time came when the Romans were looking for people to help them collect taxes from the people they ruled over. They were willing to pay. Sure, they demanded that I take a pagan oath of fidelity to the government, swearing my loyalty to Rome above all others. And I knew that I would have to sacrifice to pagan gods. But it seemed a small price to pay to become a wealthy man–someone who could really do something.

So I took the plunge and signed up to be a tax collector. I started out as your run-of-the mill guy. It was my job to go around to my people and demand they pay taxes to the government. I was responsible to pay their amount to the government, and anything I collected over that I got to keep. There wasn't a lot of accountability, so I took what I could get. Soon I had a lot of money, and I'd also had a lot of success in getting people to pay up. It wasn't long before I became the chief tax collector in my city of Jericho.

I'm sure that you can imagine that I wasn't well-liked. Nobody was glad to see me when I stopped by their home to demand payment. And I suppose that the way I dressed and carried myself made me stand out. In reality, everyone knew who I was, and I was hated. I didn't let that stop me from doing what I needed to or even what I wanted to. I know that when I walked down the street, I walked like I owned the place. I'm sure that I was deeply resented.

So anyway, I heard that Jesus was in town. Like the rest of my people, I'd heard about him. I'd heard about his miracles, and I'd heard about his claims. I truly wanted to see if he was who we all

54

thought he was. Even though I'd become a rich man because of the Romans, I would have been thrilled to see the Messiah come and throw off the bonds of our oppression. So I wanted to see him.

When I saw the crowds, I became really excited. I was surprised by the depth of my hope, actually. I thought I'd given it up when I got my job. But it was still there, lying dormant. As I looked at the crowds of people clamoring around Jesus, it wasn't long before I realized I'd never be able to see Jesus past the crowd. I'm a short man, you know. I have to make up for that in other ways.

So anyway, I saw the crowd and I made my plan. I found a tree and climbed up it. Silly, I know. We don't really climb trees. But I just wanted a glimpse of this man. So imagine my surprise when he walked up to my tree, looked me straight in the eyes, and said, "Zacchaeus, come down immediately. I must stay at your house today."†

My house? A Jew should by all rights not ever step foot anywhere near my house. I was a traitor, one who betrayed my own people. But as I looked into his eyes, I saw that he meant it. He really meant to spend the day at my house. So I shook my head and made my way down the tree.

I overheard the people then, murmuring and complaining to one another, "He has gone to be the guest of a sinner."†

I couldn't blame them, really. In their minds, I was the worst of the worst. And truly, if this was really the Messiah, I was the worst of the worst. How could I have abandoned my people and our hope? How could I have abandoned my God? I deeply regretted my decisions, and before I knew it, I said, "Look, Lord! Here and now I give half of my possessions to the poor, and if I have cheated anybody out of anything, I will pay back four times the amount."† It was absurd! And yet I found I truly meant it.

Jesus simply replied, "Today salvation has come to this house, because this man, too, is a son of Abraham. For the Son of Man came to seek and to save the lost."†

And I truly had lost my way. I had abandoned what I knew to be true and right and took my own needs and desires and made them most important in my life. But that encounter with Jesus changed me. It made me want to set things right. More than that, I wanted to be like Jesus. So instead of just following the law of Moses and returning only what I stole and hoarded, I wanted to give abundantly to the poor and return to people much more than I had taken.

So I spent that day with Jesus. And then I spent the next few years going over my accounts and finding out whom I had cheated and by how much. I did pay them back, every penny, and more, and the rest of my money I gave to the poor. I have to say that I have never regretted a day of it. Not a single day.

_____

†Quotations taken from Luke 19.

Zacchaeus's story can be found in Luke 19.

Discussion Questions

- What did you notice about this story for the first time?
- What did you wonder about?

- Why do you think Zacchaeus became a tax collector in the first place?
- Do you think he was happy with his choice?
- What do you think his relationship was with his possessions?
- Why do you think he cheated his people by charging them more?
- How do you imagine he treated the poor? How about the people he collected taxes from?

- Why do you think he wanted to see Jesus?
- What was he hoping for?
- Why do you think Jesus came over to him? Why do you think that Jesus went to his house?

- What does it mean that Jesus came to seek and to save the lost?
- What do you think he meant when he said that Zacchaeus was lost?
- Why do you think Jesus wanted to spend time with him rather than the religious people?

- What do you think prompted Zacchaeus's change of heart?
- Why do you think his encounter with Jesus led him to give back what he'd stolen?
- Why four times as much?

- What do you think it was like as he went through that process of paying people back?
- Do you think his relationship with his people changed?
- What about his relationship with Rome?
- Why was he willing to risk all those changes?
- What prompted him to give to the poor?

- How do you think greed affects a person's ability or desire to follow Jesus?
- What is it about Jesus that would make Zacchaeus respond so extravagantly?

How is Jesus changing your life? How do you want
him to change your life?

Cleopas

His was a death much like any other. It was time standing still, but careening so fast that it was all I could do to brace myself and hold on. It was pure disbelief, thinking that what I heard and saw could not be true. It was horror and despondency. It was recurring pictures in my mind of his brutal death on that despicable cross. It was the end of life as I knew it.

And yet it was more than that, too, because it was the death of everything I'd hoped for myself, my family, and my people. I believed, I truly believed, that he was the hope of Israel, the one we were waiting for. When he sent me and almost 100 others out to bear witness and tell of the coming of the kingdom of God, we saw healing and miracles and demons vanquished. After that, I had a nearly tangible hope that everything we'd been waiting for and looking for was finally here.

So when he died, all those dreams died too.

For the first two days, I sat waiting with his other
followers, stunned. I don't even know what we
were waiting for. Maybe to wake up from the
nightmare and have everything we hoped for come
true. No . . . I think we would have settled for
everything we remembered about Jesus. We sought
comfort, asked each other questions, and wept
together. We just could not understand–he was the
one we'd called Messiah, the Son of God. We had
worshiped him and given our entire lives to him.
And he had let us. Why did he let us do that if this
was to be the end? So we sat in disbelief and tried
to come to terms with what had happened.

Finally, the intensity of our shared grief
became too much for me. I just wanted to leave the
questions and uncertainty behind and go home to
Emmaus. But as I prepared to leave, the strangest
rumors started traveling around the group. Some
women had visited Jesus's tomb to prepare his body
for permanent burial, and his body was gone! What
could that mean?

So as I walked home with a friend, another

follower of Jesus, we couldn't escape the questions. As much as I wanted to forget, to pretend that it wasn't true, I couldn't help myself. I had to talk about it. So we talked about the miracles we'd seen–the water being turned into wine, the man born blind who gained his sight, even the man Jesus raised from the dead. We discussed Jesus's triumphant entrance into Jerusalem, just days before his death, where people were worshiping him in welcome. We talked about Judas and how he betrayed Jesus to the high priests. And we talked about Jesus's disappearing body.

As we walked on the road from Jerusalem to Emmaus, a man approached us from behind. He asked us, "What are you discussing together as you walk along?"†

We stopped abruptly and just stared at him. How could he not know what had happened? I said, "Are you the only one visiting Jerusalem who does not know the things that have happened there in these days?"†

"What things?" he asked.†

63

"About Jesus of Nazareth," I replied. "He was a prophet, powerful in word and deed before God and all the people. The chief priests and our rulers handed him over to be sentenced to death, and they crucified him; but we had hoped that he was the one who was going to redeem Israel. And what is more, it is the third day since all this took place. In addition, some of our women amazed us. They went to the tomb early this morning but didn't find his body. They came and told us that they had seen a vision of angels, who said he was alive. Then some of our companions went to the tomb and found it just as the women had said, but they did not see Jesus."†

Then the man said, "How foolish you are, and how slow to believe all that the prophets have spoken! Did not the Messiah have to suffer these things and then enter his glory?"†

And then he explained to us the story of God, like I'd never heard it explained before. He started with mankind's devastating rebellion in the garden, where people first chose to do exactly what

God told us not to. He showed us how that rebellion ruined all the important relationships in life–how it hurt our relationships with God, with each other, with our ability to know ourselves, even with our ability to take care of the land and resources we'd been given. And he told us of God's great plan, starting with his promise to Abraham, that the world would be rescued and reconciled to God. He spoke with disappointment about the people of Israel, and how the prophets were sent to call them always back to repentance and humility to walk with God, and how it was always his plan to send a Messiah through Israel–not just to save Israel from oppression by other nations, but to heal and restore all of our broken relationships. He talked about the Messiah, and how the Messiah was the rightful king of Israel–king of our hearts as well as our nation.

Even then, as he spoke with insight and wisdom, we didn't recognize him. He was with us for the rest of the journey home, and when we arrived, we begged him to stay with us. We didn't think it was safe for him to travel any further that night. So he did. And we sat together and ate. He blessed the food and he blessed us, and then he broke the bread and handed it around the table. In that moment, our eyes were opened, and we understood–it was Jesus! And just as quickly, he disappeared from our sight.

We could barely believe our own eyes, but we knew that something strange and wonderful had happened. So we rushed back to Jerusalem to tell the rest of the disciples. And when we arrived, Peter told a similar story. He had seen Jesus too! So we settled in to share all that we experienced with Jesus and all he had explained to us.

As we were still sharing and discussing what it all meant, Jesus appeared again, to us all. Some of the people gathered were very surprised and frightened, thinking he must be a ghost. But Jesus said, "Why are you troubled, and why do doubts rise in your minds? Look at my hands and my feet. It is I myself! Touch me and see; a ghost does not have flesh and bones, as you see I have."† And he showed us his hands and feet.

I heard gasps of disbelief, but the look on everyone's face was more a mixture of joy and surprise. We couldn't quite believe that it was true, but how could it not be? He stood right there in front of us!

Then he asked for something to eat, and someone gave him some boiled fish. Every last person in that room watched, holding his breath, as Jesus ate it. While he had our attention, he said, "This is what I told you while I was still with you: Everything must be fulfilled that is written about me in the Law of Moses, the Prophets and the Psalms. This is what is written: The Messiah will suffer and rise from the dead on the third day, and repentance for the forgiveness of sins will be preached in his name to all nations, beginning with Jerusalem. You are witnesses of these things. I am going to send you what my Father has promised; but stay in the city until you have been clothed with power from on high."†

And just like that, he invited us to submit to

his kingship and join his mission in restoring the relationships of the world. He called us his witnesses, and he told us that we would be preaching about repentance and forgiveness of sins to all nations, beginning right here in Jerusalem.

And I began to hope again. I began to hope that what I believed about Jesus was actually true–that he was the Messiah, sent from God to redeem Israel. But I also began to understand that that was so much bigger and more important than our political freedom. Jesus wanted to make us free on the inside. He wanted to free us from our need to be selfish and prideful and envious and hateful. He wanted to set us free to make him king in our lives and love God with all our hearts, soul, mind, and strength, and to love our neighbors as much as we love ourselves. That's what he was calling us to.

So we stayed in the city and waited. A group of Jesus's disciples watched as he was taken up into heaven in the little town of Bethany. And a little more than a week later, on the feast day of Pentecost, where we celebrated the day that God gave the law to Moses, we were gathered together. And all of a sudden, there was the sound of a great rushing wind, and what appeared to be tongues of fire rested above all of our heads. And we began speaking and sharing the good news about Jesus with all of those around us. And a miraculous thing happened–although there were Jews of many countries there, speaking all kinds of languages, when someone started to tell a story about Jesus, everyone understood, no matter what their language.

And that was the day, the day that the Holy Spirit came to fill us and empower us to speak about Jesus and to live for him, that we truly became the witnesses for Jesus that we were meant to be. Since that time, our community has had its ups and downs. Many went out from Jerusalem and went to tell others about Jesus and about all the things that he said and did. Those of us who stayed in Jerusalem lived in community, sharing meals and sharing property and worshiping together. We continue to learn what it means to every day lay down what we want and invite Jesus to lead and transform us.

---

† Quotations taken from Luke 24.
Cleopas's story can be found in Luke 10, Luke 24, and Acts 1-2.

Discussion Questions

- What did you notice about this story?
- What did you wonder about?

- Why do you think Jesus's death was so devastating to Cleopas?
- What do you think he was thinking about his future as he walked home to Emmaus?
- What possible explanations do you think he came up with for where Jesus's body was?
- Why do you think he didn't recognize Jesus as he walked along?

- What would it have been like to see Jesus alive after he had so clearly died?
- What do you think that told them about Jesus's power over death, over sin, and over brokenness?

- What kind of brokenness have you seen in the world?
- Why do you think God wanted to rescue people from this type of brokenness?
- Why do you think it took him so long to send Jesus to rescue us?
- Why do you think it took Jesus dying to rescue us?

- What does it mean to be filled with the Spirit?

- How do you think the Spirit helps Jesus's followers today?

How is Jesus inviting you to be a part of his plan to restore and reconcile the relationships of the world?

Appendix 1 - Glossary

Kingdom of God - This was a phrase that Jesus used a lot. There are entire books written about its meaning, but it seems to have a spiritual component when he was inviting people to participate in joining the kingdom of God. Jews and Christians both believe that there is coming a day when the kingdom of God will be fully established on earth. Christians believe that this happens one person at a time, as a person decides to live with Jesus as king of their life.

Messiah - This is the name for the person that Israel was waiting and hoping for to come and rescue it from its oppressors. The Jews believed (and there are prophecies in the Old Testament) that promise that Messiah was coming to deliver them. So the entire community waited (and the Jews who don't believe Jesus was Messiah still wait) for that Messiah to come and bring them deliverance.

Passover - This is the Jewish festival that celebrated the Jews' deliverance from slavery in Egypt. You can find the story of the first Passover in Exodus 12. The command for the Jews to celebrate Passover is found in Numbers 9.

Pentecost - This is a Jewish festival to celebrate the time when God gave the Jews the law on Mt. Sanai.

Pharisees - These were people in a specific sect of Judaism. They worked very hard to follow every single law that was written in the Torah. They also had made lots of other rules that expanded on those laws in the Torah, just to make sure they never even got close to breaking the law. They were very educated, and very concerned with keeping Israel set apart as God's people, prepared for the coming Messiah.

Prophet - Over the history of the Old Testament, when God had a special message for the Jews, he often sent a prophet. The prophet was given a message by God and then had to go and tell the people. Many times, the prophet would have to do some kind of activity that provided a word picture to help illustrate God's message for the people. Many of these prophets spoke of a coming Messiah who would deliver Israel from its bondage.

Rabbi - A rabbi is a Jewish teacher. Many of them had pupils, and many had disciples or followers who would listen to them and do what they said.

Reconcile - To reconcile is to make things right, usually in relationships. It's the idea of restoring something or healing a broken relationship.

Redeem - To buy or to pay for something. There's a really great story in the Old Testament that sets the stage for Jesus to be called the Redeemer. It's the story of Ruth being redeemed by her kinsman redeemer Boaz, and it's found in the Book of Ruth.

Resurrection—A rising from the dead. There are stories in the Bible where Jesus literally raises someone from the dead (like Lazarus), and there are other times that the Bible talks about raising people from spiritual death.

Ruling Council– This was the group of rulers in the Jewish world who made the religious and social laws that the Jews were supposed to follow. It was something only an educated and important person would belong to.

Sabbath Day– This was the day of rest that God commanded the Jews to have in the Ten Commandments. It was celebrated from sundown on Friday night to sundown on Saturday night. The Jews were not allowed to do any work on the Sabbath, and the Pharisees had laid out a lot of extra rules about what that meant, including that people could not carry a mat (bedroll) on the Sabbath day. They could not even lead an animal down the road.

Samaritans—These were people who were part Jew and part non-Jew. They had remained true to their belief in God, but they did not have all the same beliefs as those who were full-blooded Jews. They were looked down upon by the Jews.

Torah—Torah is the first five books of the Christian Bible—Genesis, Exodus, Leviticus, Numbers, and Deuteronomy. These are the original laws handed down by Moses to the Jewish people. They tell the Jews their history and give them a foundation of law to follow to demonstrate that they are committed to remaining true to God.

Appendix 2 – Leader's Guide

Lesson Plans

- <u>5 minutes</u> - Welcome and introduce the idea of biblical storying. Emphasize that it's important to imaginatively listen and try to put yourself in the story.
- <u>5 minutes</u> - Read the story.
- <u>10 minutes</u> - Re-tell the story. This can be as straightforward as just going around in a circle, each saying what happened next, or as elaborate as putting on a play to act it out or drawing pictures. Be creative!
- <u>25 minutes</u> - Discussion Questions. As you prepare, be prayerful about the questions that seem most relevant to your group. Always be prepared to share your own responses to the questions to kick off the group.
- <u>10 minutes</u> - Application/Journaling time. Leave art supplies out so that people can draw or write during this time. It's also a good idea to supply a journal or a folder so that people can respond to the questions, though there's also room in this book, if everyone has their own copy.
- <u>10 minutes</u> - Pray for one another.

Facilitator Notes

Nicodemus

In our test groups, there were several things that we needed to explain a little bit deeper than the story does.

Jewish Ruling Council - Nicodemus was a member of the Jewish Ruling Council. This was a group of 70 men who made day-to-day judicial and leadership decisions for the Jewish community.

Messianic Hope - In order to understand this story, it is important for participants to have some knowledge of the Jewish story, particularly about how the Jews were promised a deliverer (that they called the Messiah), and many believed that he would save them politically, from the Romans, and set up a new Jewish political kingdom.

Moses and the Serpent in the Wilderness - Numbers 21:4-9 tells the story of the Israelites in the desert complaining against God and not trusting him. As a result, there was a plague of snakes upon them, and when they cried out for deliverance, God told Moses to make a snake and put it on a pole. If the people looked on it, they would live. Jesus drew a parallel from this story to himself, foreshadowing his death on the cross.

Life with the Eternal One - I grew up learning the language of "eternal life" when we talked about what it meant to follow Jesus: If you follow him, you will have eternal life. It's very easy to misinterpret this to mean only that your spiritual life will extend after your physical death. But the meaning of eternal life is deeper, and I wanted to express that deeper meaning by explaining that when you follow Jesus you have life with the Eternal One–not only after death but also now. In the discussion after this story, that was one of the most important things I wanted people to start thinking about: What would life look like, and how would it be different if they had a relationship with the Eternal God?

Woman at the Well

Fictionalized Story - There is more imaginative material in this story than in any other of the Encounters. We don't know much of anything at all from history or Scripture about the woman at the well. Yet her conversation with Jesus is so powerful. The dialogue is faithful to the scriptural account. But make sure the participants know that they won't see access to her motivations or thoughts in the Bible.

Blind Man

Faith Versus Doubt and Fear - This story naturally leads to a discussion of what it means to step out by faith and how you do that even in the face of fear or doubt. Take some time to discuss how what we think about Jesus makes us feel about Jesus and how that affects what we do about Jesus's invitations to us.

Hearing Jesus - Unlike the blind man, we don't interact with Jesus in physical form. How do we hear him or see what he's doing? How do we know what he's asking us to do? Use your life and your experience with Jesus to model what that can look like in a Christian's life.

Rich Young Ruler

Belief in Jesus - This was the most disturbing of all the Encounters stories for my group participants who had not yet chosen to follow Jesus. Here, it's really important to talk about what belief is. Rather than being an intellectual assent to a list of beliefs, it needs to be understood as including our actions. It's not enough to believe that Jesus existed or even that he is God. Jesus demands something from us.

It's easy here to move into trying to define, based on external factors, whether someone believes in Jesus. Instead of that, try to focus on how true faith requires expression, and expression of faith in Jesus means obedience to him.

Martha

Jesus Wept - Spend some time imagining why Jesus wept at Lazarus's death. Did he not know he was going to raise Lazarus from the dead? Some commentaries say that he may have been weeping at the brokenness of the world and how far away from God's intentions that brokenness is. What might it mean if God is sad about the state of the world and about death?

Zacchaeus

Transformation - Talk about what it looks like to be transformed by Jesus. Zacchaeus's life was totally and utterly changed by his meeting with Jesus. How has transformation happened in your own life and what kinds of transformation do people want to ask Jesus for?

Cleopas

Invitation to the Kingdom - The main focus of this story is on the invitation to join Jesus in his work of restoring and redeeming the world. If Jesus is transforming and making you whole, then he is not doing that just for your own benefit–he also wants to use you in transforming and restoring the world. If he is sad about the brokenness of the world, then we as his people are sent to begin to help heal the broken relationships and systems that are around us. Encourage your participants to imagine what part they can play in Jesus's kingdom work.

About the Author

Anna Rapa has been following Jesus for more than 30 years, and she has shared the stories of Jesus with many people of many different cultures. She wrote Encounters with Jesus for a group of her friends, and she saw their lives transformed as they encountered Jesus when they read and responded to these stories together. She is praying that, through these stories, you will encounter Jesus too.

Anna welcomes comments or questions at her personal website, www.annarapa.com or at her email, annarapa@gmail.com.

.

Also available from Da[w]bar House Press:

Alex Cunningham's recent motorcycle accident changed his life–now he sees every day as a mission to share the good news of the gospel. But his long-time girlfriend, Annie Russo, just doesn't understand. And if that isn't enough, every time Alex opens his mouth to say something about God at work, everything backfires: his co-manager Drew rarely even looks at him now.

But help comes in the form of Sara Locke, an ex-missionary widow with wisdom to share. Together, Alex, Annie, and Sara discover how to see people's unspoken emotional barriers to faith in God. Along the way, Alex and Annie explore how to engage those barriers in natural and nonjudgmental ways as they begin to talk about their Christian faith with their friends. But one of them has more success than the other, and the stress on their relationship might just be too much.

A new blend of fiction and evangelism training, author Anna Rapa uses narrative storytelling to communicate key truths about evangelism in today's postmodern world. Dive into the story of Alex and Annie, and let this story show you how to reach people in today's culture with God's transforming story of rescue.

19893636R00050

Made in the USA
Charleston, SC
16 June 2013